AF477554

Dedication:

I dedicate this book to my dear friend, Tajalli, all my teachers, including my family, especially my children and grandchildren.

"Welcome the present moment as if you had invited it. It is all we ever have so we might as well work with it instead of struggle against it. We might as well make it our friend and teacher rather than our enemy."
- Pema Chodron

"Take Refuge in the Present Moment"
- Thich Nhat Hanh

Aspiration:

May this book benefit you and all sentient beings

Special thanks to Greg....
who was great to work with on this project!

NOW

round and round we go tick tock round the clock minute by minute round

Dakini Lynn Marlow

Preface to 2nd edition:

I've added some new poems to this edition as well as a few photographs. The photos are visual poems. Please "read" them as such. Most people, when they look at art want to know what it is. The mind asks: "what am I looking at?" It tries to "make sense" of it. My photos are meditations, poetic meditations, brought forth from the imaginal world to the liminal one, not the concrete one.

I invite you to "see" if you can put aside that inquiring pre frontal cortex and instead of actively looking at the image before you, take a few moments to open your eyes and receive the image. And "feel" what the image evokes in you. Sometimes when I see a piece of art that really moves me, I actually salivate. It' s a visceral response. Be open to surprises! Sometimes a message might appear, an unbidden creature, an angel or..... you tell me.... might appear.

You may also use these images to write your own poem in the space left at the end of the book or in your own journal. You can experiment, starting with: "Now I see....' And "see what comes!

I've also added a visual sense with the spacing of the words and lines of the poems. So you might just take a moment in some cases and see the wholeness of the poem. This is not totally random, spontaneous mainly, but arising out of re-reading the poems and listening to the spaces. Give time to the spaces, feel the words. Let them carry you along a river of nows!

Introduction

"Be in the now!"
"Be present! "
"Let go of the past."
"Don't worry about the future."

Well that is all good advice. No doubt about it. Sages have been saying it for eons. Ram Das said it "back in the day" in his epic book from the sixties: Be Here Now!

Life IS a series of "Now's," each with its narrative, thoughts, and feelings. That's what makes life – well life. We have experiences. We interact. Thoughts and feelings naturally follow. Depending on how we feel and therefore what we think (and vice versa,) we assign meaning and based on our interpretation, we make a decision and choose to act this way or that- one Now at a time, now after now - which leads to the next experience: over and over. That's our life.

Sometimes being here now is natural, even a joy. The moment is pleasant and even glorious. In fact, there are times when we absolutely savor the moment. But how about those now's that are painful, terrifying, devastating? Think: life threatening for ourselves or those we are close to. And then there are the global events we are all too familiar with that can be shattering. Some moments suck all the life energy out of us.

Being in the present sometimes means being with the painful feelings, and finding a way to digest and metabolize them so that we can grow in wisdom, strength, courage, insight, love, and compassion.

But, I ask you, is it realistic to expect ourselves to over-ride the workings of our physiology? It is natural – human - to become desperate and our immediate impulse is to do whatever we can to escape the pain of the moment and avoid being present. Our neurotransmitters start rapid firing, muscles tense, it's hard to breathe. At these times, our fight, flight, flee adrenaline soaked body freaks out and we may actually disassociate. The current trauma exponentially triggers impressions of past trauma. Sometimes, even without the actual memories, only body memories, from our past naturally bleed into the present and our ability to "be here now" is drained and we are driven to do anything to escape the moment..

So we see, we know from experience, that sometimes, this approach, to "be here now," although great if you can get it, do it, is not within our abilities. The pain is agonizing and unfortunately, not tolerable. We try counting our breaths, yoga, running, weight lifting, etc. but to no avail. Our body hurts. Our thoughts are like tigers pacing madly in a small cage. Our heart breaks. We are in shock!

When the feelings flood us, is it really possible to "let go?" Is it possible to "be present?" Can we tolerate the pain, anger, fear – the combination of all three plus – to access the qualities and capacities we need to live in the Now and the Here, negotiate life's trajectory without being overwhelmed by the past and therefore worry and dread of the future?

How do we withstand the temptation, the overarching compelling need to find some way of escape, through drugs, alcohol, psychiatric medication, workaholism? There are an infinite number of methods on hand. Choose your poison as some say.

It can be a life long challenge to shed the residue of trauma, to heal. The scars cut deep and can be crippling. Over and over throughout some of our lives, we find ourselves stymied, derailed, and unable to fulfill our dreams, or even "simply" find some ease NOW and then.

So one day with the intention of practicing being more present, I started saying to myself, "Now..." and writing down what came. This practice helps me cultivate my ability to be here now at various times during the day when I may be running around, busy with life's tasks and especially when the stress is high. It helps me to come to my senses! Literally! When I think: "Now," I bring my awareness to my senses, Now, I see, now I hear, now I smell, etc. This helps me to refocus. And it's not necessarily some cosmic experience. It's very simple:

Now
I am brushing my teeth,
now I am seeing the sky.
Now I am hearing...

In those sweet moments when life is good, it helps me
deepen and relax and savor the moment. And when the
times are tough, it doesn't always mean that the pain, the
grief, the anxiety stop, but it seems to some times put all
that in context and give me a handle, something to hold
on to (and let go of) and I am able to be with myself, my
feelings and sensations, to one degree or another, and not
just run around obsessed by whatever is causing the distur-
bance.

So I offer you these poems with the intention that you
too may find your way to live your life more fully. I offer you
these poems with the hope that you may find your way to
be with your experiences, to be with your feelings, to honor
them, to wholeheartedly "Be HERE NOW!" as Ram Das said.

Blessings to you in this Now!

NOWNOWNOWNOWNOWNOWNOWNOWNOWNOW **NOW** NOWNOWNOWNOWNOWNOWNOWNOWNOW

now
        the question
                                arises
shall I date these nows
                and I think
why?
        they are all
now
-
what is now?
        you ask
        I ask
now
        is
the winter mountain sun
        casting warmth
light on my chilled face
        illuminating the darkness
                behind my closed eye lids
light on the water
        frothing   and   sliding
curling   and   dappling
an invisible dog barking
                                staccato
                                punctuating
the song of the waterfall
                                in this

one   unceasing   transient

                          now

-

now
what is now
when is now
the cusp between
this and that
between here and there
now
a Zen moment
on the dock
on the shore
between land and sea
between you and me
between pain and joy
between days of breath
and the inevitable
now
of No
Breath

-

now
I'm thinking
that's what minds do
they think
thought full

no one wants to be
thought less
mind full
or might it be
mind (the thoughts) less
how about
be
heart full
may our minds be
full of thoughts
of Love
what does it mean
any way
to be
mind full
full of thoughts
or
the opposite
no thoughts
now
that's a thought
-
now is
    the here
        and the there
some times
    now is

here
for a moment
        and in the next moment
here   becomes   t
            There
and the questions
                    that arise
the how's and the why's
and the what happens next
as we see and we hear
we taste and we smell
we sense and we feel
we laugh and we cry
we try
        and we get by
                moment   by   moment
now
-
how now!?
no one really knows
hardly anyone asks
what do you think?
-
why now
people almost always ask that
why now?
why me?

how did we come to be?
what will happen next?
will I be happy
will I be sad
will I be here
or there?
and when?
when will it end?
how will it be?
and what does it all mean?
is it up to you and me,
my friend?
so what to you think?
now
-
now
     once in a life time
          over and over
all the same
      all different
          yet
only   one
     now
how could that be?
-
     now sitting on a picnic table bench
  in the park   by the creek

a little girl
                leaps for a frisbe
carried   in   a   far
                            arc
                                        by the wind
arms   s t r e t c h e d   to   the
                limit
                                        she runs
as fast as her little legs can carry her
                            skirt rising
                        hair blowin
            she rolls on the grass
        grabs hold
                    laughs
        under the afternoon sun

-

another now
                                        here
        in the mid day sun
        a prayer of gratitude
                    in my heart
                    now

-

now
a warm bronze sun
rests
a halo on

top of a mountain peak
the wind blows
and the river flows
singing and dancing
to the sea
inside and outside
you and me
and all that be's
as bombs fall
children starve
husbands and wives quarrel
politicians squabble
democracy unravels
corporations infallible
the earth turns in its orbit
how could that be
now

-

here now
in my studio
on the deep red velour couch
writing to you
where are you
now?

-

now
since you are so far away

I will have to find a way
to feel
as I would
if you were here
safe and warm
in your arms
my heart and soul
in a reverie of
sweet cream honey
and the light of our smiles
squinting through our eyes
glints and glows
I rest my head
on the shore of your breast
my palm warming your heart
waves of love
ooze and throb
over my bare body
I glide and slide
in the tide of your touch
the tips of your fingers
so soft and kind
A lightness so tender
it reaches fathoms deep
opens and quickens
the longing lavishing
in the sacred cave

of my heart womb
together we
flare
burst into flame
all around
and belly laugh outloud
we hold each other
tight
through the night
awake to a sweet dawn
that blossoms into sun rise
arms and legs entwined
then dance our way
through the day
in our own special way
-
now
driving down the road
signaling left
signaling right
destination in sight
spring in the air
now arriving
here in the sunlight
here in the breeze
I dance with the trees
fly with the birds

roar with lions
I thunder
I fire breathing dragon
blaze
with Kali*

     I   out   rage
and   I   praise

-

now
on the beach
by the sea
gentle breeze
clear skies
with wisps of clouds floating by
me alone with You
as the sun sets

-

now
the night storm has passed
I open my eyes
and see
the clear blue sky
a new day

-

now
already come and gone
a new now

again and again
now

-

now
I am hungry
now
I am sad
now I laugh
now I dance
this now

-

now
    I am not
        alone
for You are here
     and all there is
        is   here
and everywhere I be
    is
    Love

-

now
I want to write about grief
nothing as beautiful
as pure grief
a place where
love and pain are inseparably woven

with ultra fine gold tendrils
a basket of memories
hopes and fears
and of course
an ocean of tears
-
now
closer deeper steeper
take your time
slowly slide
breath by breath
one now at a time
let your mind chatter
chatter on
shift your gaze
from the morass and the maze
be a cat
snuggling in my lap
feel the thought bees
buzzing in your heart hive
let them pollinate and light up your face
rest in silver silence
on the shore of here and now
-
now
I awake
dark

NOW

of night
my mind an anthill
thoughts
scurrying around
moving bits
here and there
as I turn
this way and that
-

now
if only
this now
could be forever
and other nows
never
-

now
I am looking
into your eyes
as the palms of your hands
cradle my face
love now
-

now the sound of the gong
      resounds   in my heart
                      echoes
echoes   echoes   echoes

now   now   now

    now   now

-

now
a moment of peace
a moment of joy
thought less
only heart beat
and breath
the echo of the gong

-

now

    fades

      into

        then

          and

        ambles

      on

     to

  when

then   returns   to   here

and
boomerangs   back to   there
    again and again
from   now   to   now

-

now
inhale
now
exhale
now
heart beats
now blood flows
eyes see
ears hear
and a smile appears
now
-
now
a sigh
now
a tear
now
an embrace
ah! Now
-
that now
I forget
this now
I remember
now home
now lost
but not forever

-

now
        union with my consort
lips   and   tongues
                glide and slide
arms and legs
                entwined
so fine
-

now
in front of the altar
of divine union
obsidian and quartz crystal
candle burns
scent of sage
rises
now
communion
-

now
fly with the angels
far above
below
a sea on fire
your lips caress my cheek
I become
pure desire

-

now
the pain thief
taunts me
steals my joy
robs me of days
threatens life
a reminder
only a limited number
of nows
until the final
Then

-

now
lying in the lounge chair
basking in sunlight
under the old apple tree
in my garden
convalescing from visceral grip
praising health

-

thankful for a pain free now
sunny summer day
in early spring
a walk through the neighborhood
violet Crocuses rise out of crusty snow

-

now
      I   am   not
                        Alone
for   You   are   here
      and   all   there Is
         Is
         Love
-

now
hands tell a story
of hard work love and glory
a woman of light and sight
she always finds her way
to make it
through the day
heart and eyes open
wondering
"what's the story?"
where is my Be Longing
knowing
still
Love
all ways
-

now
I decide
to go

NOW

this way
or that
where will it lead me?
the next now
-
now
I
ask
can love prevail
or will fear derail
some times
it's literally
touch and go
still
I pray
it will stay
a few more nows
-
now
Shiva's* got me by the balls
Kali*
by the hair
while
Tara* sits
on the lotus
in my
heart

-

now
I am
now
I can
then I did
this now
I will

-

now
let's pray
for the trees
dance for the bees
bow to
our scorched and aching earth
we weep and we wail
we sing and we dance
weaving our brokenness
whole
life will prevail

-

now
all I have
one after another
there can be no other
all the rest
hopes and dreams

memories and visions
-
now
memories and visions
abound
I laugh and I cry
they whirl around
inside what's called my mind
I do not know where it exists
in time and space
is there any other place?
-
now
only breath
dissolving into breeze
this inhale
that exhale
breathe the breath of trees
and seas
now
it's time for
imagination
to take flight
into gardens of delight
to far off shores
secret amethyst caves
with mermaids and water falls

lions and dolphins
nuns and monks and
corporate thieves
shamans and angels
dancing and singing
together
-

now
I hear
advice
blaring through
the car radio
                    "never get discouraged
                              never give up"
          sometimes
          easier said
          than done
-

now
I wake up
a deep night's sleep
slips away
now
a bright blue sky
sunlight flies
through the windows
of my eyes

but alas
a wave of sadness
grief for
lost love laughter and song
washes up on the dawn of my joy
can't stop the tide of tears that glide by
still
I wonder
how
why
and wish it were a wave of bliss
a hug and a kiss
a smile and a snuggle
now
only a memory
-
now
I want to tell you
about my life
there is so much to tell
and I don't know where to begin
I do know
where it began
and when
so much has happened
since then
some times

it feels
like
it's been so long
some times
only
a moment
but
here I am
still
now
a grandmother
with stories to tell
songs to sing
tickles and cuddles
the most important things
what more is there to say
time to play
-
is now
the time
to say goodbye
and thanks for everything
all the laughter
all the adventures
tender moments
hot baths
blazing fires

kisses and caresses
love and faith
outdone by fear and doubt
what happened to "love conquers all?"
I've learned so much
and sad though I feel
longing lives on
you were a surprise
but was it all a disguise
such sweet names
precious angel
beloved
but push came to shove
love hit a wall in the relation ship maze
you turned back
I am prepared to go on
who knows what next will appear
in one of the nows to come
-
now
on the bench
by the sea
wondering
what's the next surprise
I look up
Vilma appears
he has a story to tell

"about my life"
he begins,
"I was born in Ethiopia
I have traveled far:
a poet with a speech defect
crippled by cerebral palsy
"still" he says,
"I cry out against injustice
I do not turn my eye
or try to sweeten the pie
I say it like it is
painful though it is to hear
Africa My Home!"
-
now
I
await
cosmic cervix
about to open
contractions
rapid and strong
I know in my bones
what it means
to be reborn
the second birth
does not have to echo
the first

that's redemption
the soul's journey
from seed
to sprout
to stem branch and leaf
and finally
full bloom
to seed again
-

now
I realize
it can't happen
with ambivalence
hard enough
with a whole heart
not a half
I think of Dorothy
her journey with the heartless lion
love demands Courage
-

am I not
now
Kurukule*
with her bow and arrow
made of flowers
pulled back taut
she is just about to release her bow

and see that arrow fly
only to pierce
the bull's eye
in my heart
at the core
when it hits its mark
the flowers explode
and each petal
shape shifts
into fireworks and butterflies
and I become
pure
love
-
now
sitting on the dock
at the harbor
down under
Antarctica
a breath away
but here now
a warm sunny day
sun shining
clear blue sky
gentle breeze
can you feel it
tossling your hair

caressing your cheeks
the scent of sea
a starfish at your feet
black clams
gripping a wall
one on top
of the other
dead or alive
I wonder

-

now
green hills
embrace
homes and shops
people on skateboards
people on bikes
children in playgrounds
swimming and kayaking
lovers with lattes and cappuccinos
teens diving off the peer
climbing up
dripping shivering
hugging themselves dry
laughing and daring
so totally in the Now

-

now news

9.2 earthquake
tsunami warnings too
shook Santiago
and all of Chile
children asleep in their beds
grand parents in wheelchairs
shoeless homeless
doctors lawyers
all sentient beings trembled in awe
racing for solid ground
afraid to be swallowed up by monster tidal
waves
if not me
who
could be
mother father
baby brother
definitely some one's
sister wife cousin daughter
like Humpty Dumpty
we are in the midst of a great fall
our shell will shatter
what will emerge
now?
–

now
another grave tragedy

more gripping grief to carry
but life still lives
clawing aching hunger
an emptiness that
feels like it can never be filled
I bear witness
the least I can offer
I open my arms
embrace life
all those loved ones
lost
all those whose hearts have been broken
I bow to you
palm to palm
I proffer a prayer
a prayer for Grace
mercy mercy mercy
-
now
sitting
now
writing
now
walking
now
taking pictures
now

sun playing with water and air
now
free from clouds
unobscured
warmth and light
prevail
-

now by now
history happens
to be either forgotten distorted or
remembered
now and then
-

now
                    a bridge
between   birth   and   death
                    only now
          one   after   another
-

now
I am shocked
it's hard to believe
but it is actually true
worry doubt and fear
have disappeared
vanished
but not all of a sudden

years and years
of crossing out and erasing
reshaping and reforming
but finally
I realize
right now
I am excited about the future
open to surprise
seems so natural
sitting at the cool café
on Wellington Bay
cappuccino
pen notebook camera
on hand
ready
what now!
-
now
I come home
to my Self
with open arms
open heart
only love
welcome!
-
now
at the chocolate factory Café

on a misty rainy day
I'm wending my way
-

now
I write
to heal my heart
a cauldron on fire
bubbling broth
with no turmeric or salt
a dash of melted dreams
a fistful of frozen fears
a tablespoon of tears
a cup of wilted red roses
thorns and all
a healthy helping
of hug fruit
a splash of smile syrup
let it simmer
all through the night
and it will feed me
for life
-

now
I sit on the isle of Avalon
I gaze into the well
I await the oracle
I am here

speak to me
-
now
I stand my ground
I refuse to be derailed
detained deflated
"steady"
Sophia* says
to my nervous system
"easy does it"
close your eyes
take a breath
reset
reboot
express train
on the destiny track
whiz along
cruisn' on down the line
a now at a time
-
now
I am resurfacing
from a journey to the underworld
I passed through many gates
I let go of so much
so much taken from me
many sacrifices

Love home peace freedom
I did not think I would survive
fear anger pain
overwhelmed
held down
alone
cold hungry soul
but like Inanna*
I prevailed
I found determination
strength and courage
I didn't know I had
blessed with friends and family
now I return
to share
the hidden gifts of the underworld
for those who dare
-

    now
miles   and   miles   and   miles
of windmills
    on the spine of Aeoterea*
    wings silently circling
-

now
my soul's on fire
longing

for a pool of deliciousness
now
I can relax
all that I have longed for
my heart's desire
is now
-
now
I am a cloud
now pouring rain
whipping wind
now
a volcano
river of molten lava
sea on fire
sunset on mountain top
candle flame
on the altar
of now
-
now
I am
putting the dishes away
my heart a pressure cooker
all the elements churning
heart pumps
lungs breathe

stay
stay with it
bear it
ride it like a bronco
ride it like a tidal wave
ride it like Neytiri rides her Thanator
brave wise skillful
until
back home to another now
putting the dishes away
-
now
there is no other way
nothing else to do
but
surrender
like the fool*
on one toe
dangling over the cliff
not light hearted with a flower in my mouth
more like gritting my teeth
as I wobble on the edge
on the cliff of now
as Gaia is
raped pillaged and poisoned
corporate terrorists
have their way with us

we are fracked!
genetically modified
to become part of the consumer Borg
will humans be turned into drones
with numbers instead of names
or will   .....
-
now
just You listen to me
yes YOU
I'm talking to You
Big You
the one and only You
inside outside
everything
Sophia
awesome mystery
protect us
guide us
into the heart of hearts
please
now!
-
now
it's time
to check in with your Self
stop

look and listen
what do you see
what do you hear?
how do you feel?
-

now
I'm walkin'
yes indeed I am walkin'
singin' a song
walkin' my little girl
back home
we're skipping and giggling
making funny faces
being butterflies and balloons
flyin' around
another sunny day
in the garden
no need to worry or hurry
-

now
I turn to
the one
inside me who wants to be born
I feel her heart
beat strong
sure and determined
she knows what she wants

knows how to get it
knows she can get it
by giving it
so she lies back
closes her eyes
breathes in all the way
until it turns
right around
and flows out
-
now
do I dare
show you
who I am
if I could
would you
recognize her
have the eyes to see
the heart to hear and feel
how do I know
you will care
and not judge me out of hand
maybe you won't understand
or simply ignore
turn around and walk out the door
do as you may
but I do believe

it s best
to be kind
-
now
       I understand
now
       I know
now
       I see
now
       now
sunshine
       now
rain
       now
too hot
       now
too cold
       now
pain
       now
pleasure
       now
anger
       now
Love!
-

now
I close my eyes
breathe into my heart
sigh
I see the little one
inside
she cries
so much hurt
so much fear
no one there
how can she forget
how can she trust
remember remember
that was then
this is now
-
now
vibrant colors
splash shapes
curl and swirl
here and there
this way and that
no holding back
-
now
a cracked heart
dripping crimson

encased in grey squares
squeezed to death
by betrayals and lies
a prayer
redemption
now

-

now
so many worrisome possibilities
disasters
dangling by a thread
waiting for a gentle breeze
for an axe to fall
breaking my heart
death of a loved one
loss of love
crippling my body
economic
environmental disaster
possibilities are endless
redemption…. inevitable?

-

now
I believe
all will be well
I will thrive
no need for abortion

no miscarriage
no birth trauma
Tara*
Swift Savioress
abides
-

now
I am ready
deeper
settle deeper
eyes close
breath happens
stewing
my soul
being stirred
in the cauldron
of creation
in the bubbling brew
life on planet earth
-

now
the planet is cooking
choking and drowning
in toxic waste
why are we all
acting
so calm cool and collected

why not
as Dylan Thomas once said
"rage rage against the dying of the light!"
-

Kurukule*
pull back your bow
aim your arrow made of flowers
at the frozen hearts
and sotted minds
that trod on
the rights of
love and beauty
Kali* Rising,
Durga* come now
riding your tiger
with your retinue of Dakinis*
vanquish injustice and corruption
-

what color is now?
now is a rainbow
now comes in many colors
an infinite number of hues
shades and textures
her sounds span
from pianissimo
the softest whispers
to the greatest fortissimo

NOW

-
what else
is there
to do
now
but
sit here
in the shade
of the cottonwoods
draping the ribbon of river
trickling and tumbling
down
the Sangre de Cristos pass
invisible breath
whirls the cotton
fairies dancing
like fire flies
Georgia O'Keefe sky
above
inside
a sea of tears
in my heart
of years
gone by
thrusts through
the canal
spanning heart

and eyes
cloud covered
but dry
and
the thunderous rage
batters the dam
in my mind
only a mute prayer
who knows how
who knows where
as Jesus in the olive garden
"may this cup pass…"
-
now
    time in
       in time
   and space
  a Point of Stillness*
in the Breath of LIfe
  no worry about
    how or why
 what to do
which way to go
  what's it all about
    this one and only moment
  a drop splashing in the Tide
of Primary Respiration

glinting silver in the clear blue sky
shapeshifts into a star
that flashes for an instant
and then
is
simply gone
beyond
here
now
-
now
it's time
to check in with your Self

s t o p

look
listen
what do you see?
-

now
solitude   and   silence
are my refuge
now
incense wafts pungent and sweet
candlelight's
warm golden glow

licks my face
all reminding me to listen
                              hush
shh!
the angels are singing my song
and that's   all   there   is   to
know
grateful   for   this   and   every
so   very   precious
                  moment
the   blessings   flow
                          some moments
are harder to claim as   Refuge
some times   it's life in a war zone
some times   impossible
to recognize the angels
        when rain is pounding
cold winds
        twisting   turning   slashing
pounding
fog so thick
visibility nil
devastating drought
        volcanos erupting
deceived by betrayals and lies
                          but even then
I try

           to find refuge
with the angels always by my side
-

now
cradled in my hammock
womb wrapped
gently swinging
as day slips
into dusk
steel grey clouds
            hug peaks
         thunder growls
inevitably
      lightening flashes
here
then who knows   where
thunder rolls over
                 and over
the porch roof
quakes
            still
not   a drop   falls from above
although   the breeze
chills
pungent   with the succulent scent of rain
is that You, Beloved?

            -

now
Bast *
the Egyptian cat goddess

           appears
with her feline wisdom
    head held high
    heart open wide
    arms radiating glory
independent
sure of foot
lanky
    leaping
        clawing
scratching
    curling
        and unfurling
reminding me
        to slide
and
    glide
        s t r e t ch
    and   roll
                    and
above   all

be bold!

-

now
my eyes close
I rest
my head in my hands
my heart drums on
breath waves roll over and over
"hush baby girl
don't you cry

          mama's gonna sing you
     a lullaby"
not rock-a-bye baby
no cradle will fall
so there's nothing to fear
"rest your sweet face
on my breast
I hold you near and dear"
-

now
    is
already
    then
then
    again
     (when?)
now is

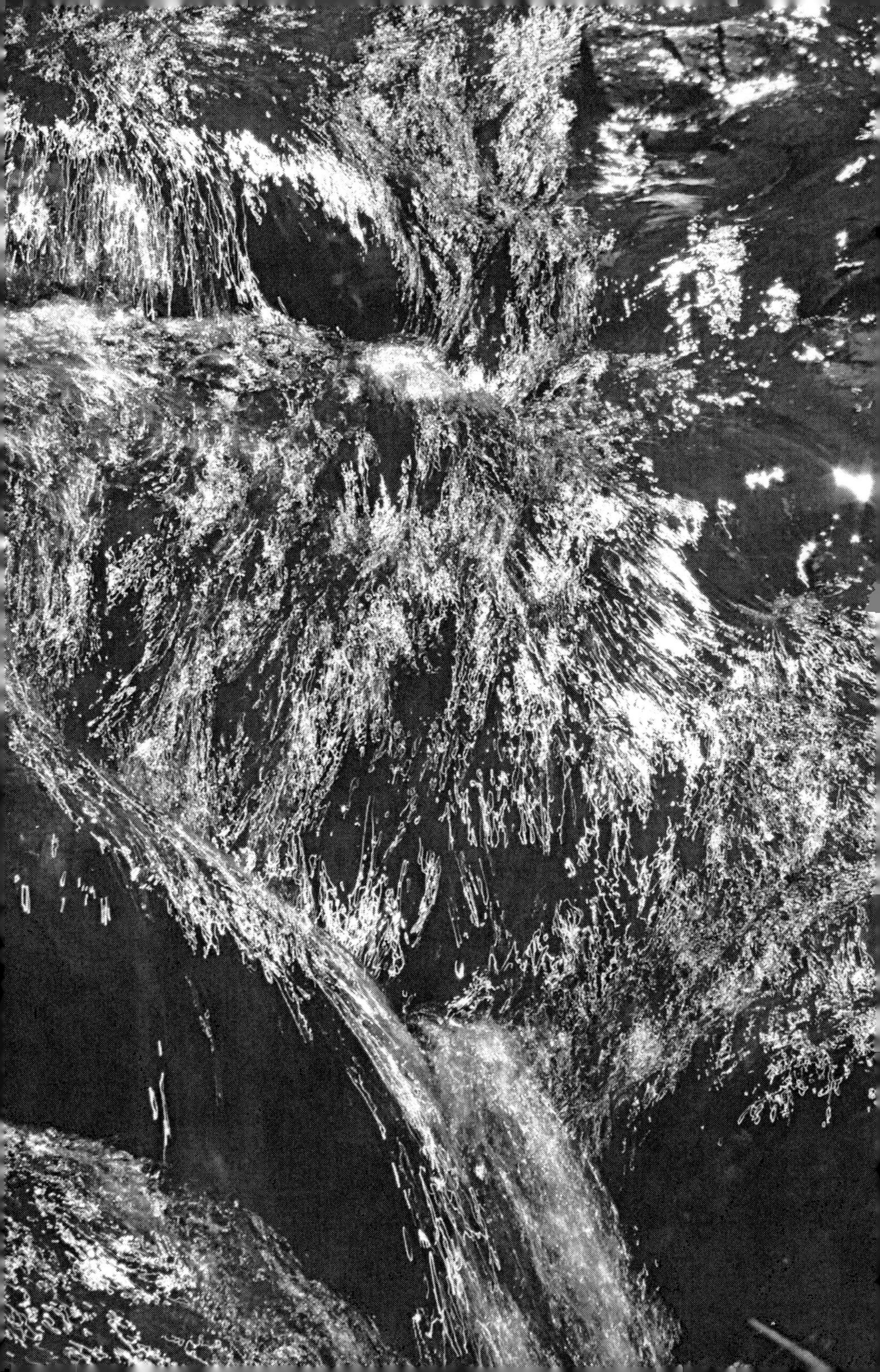

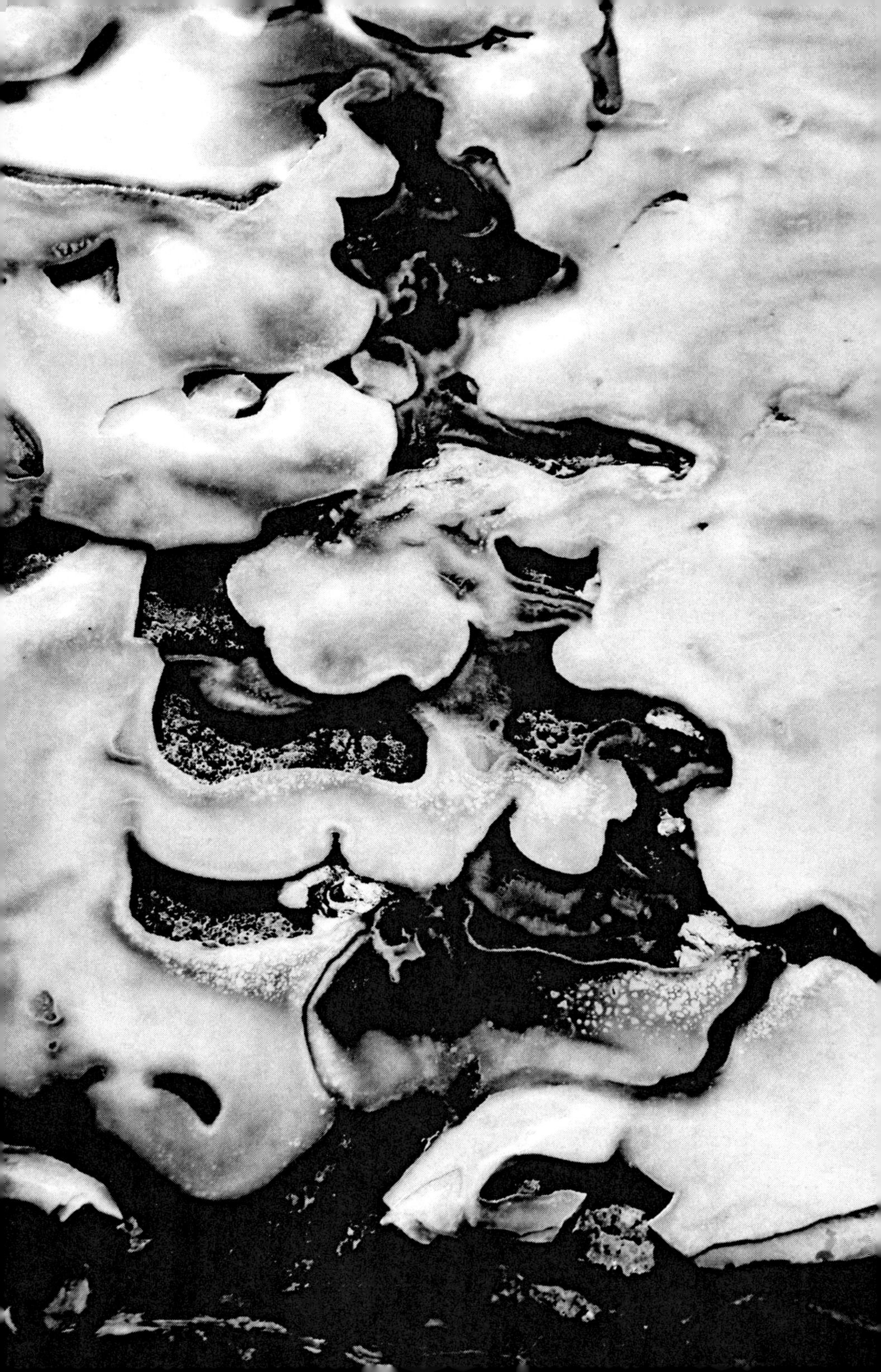

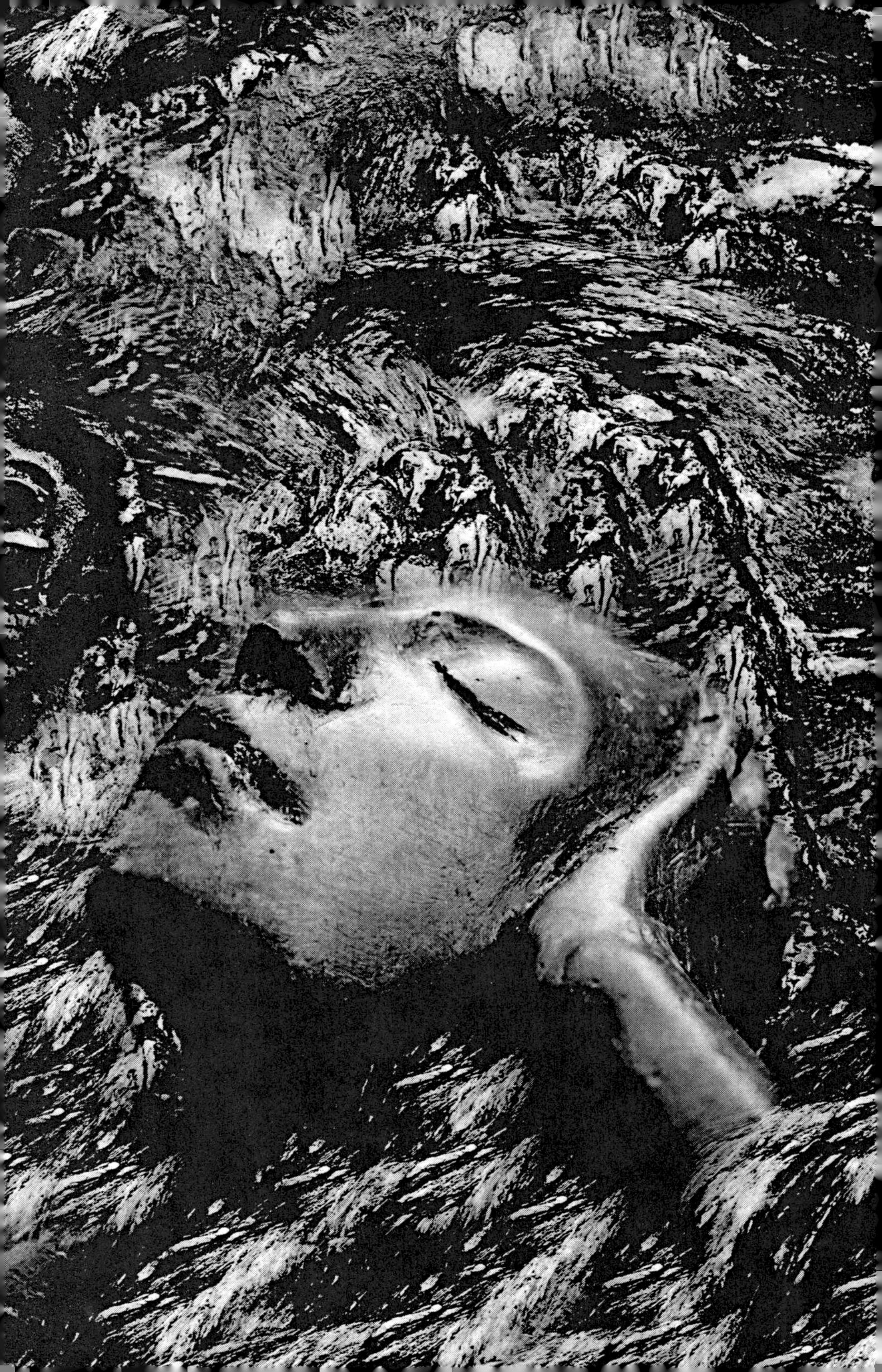

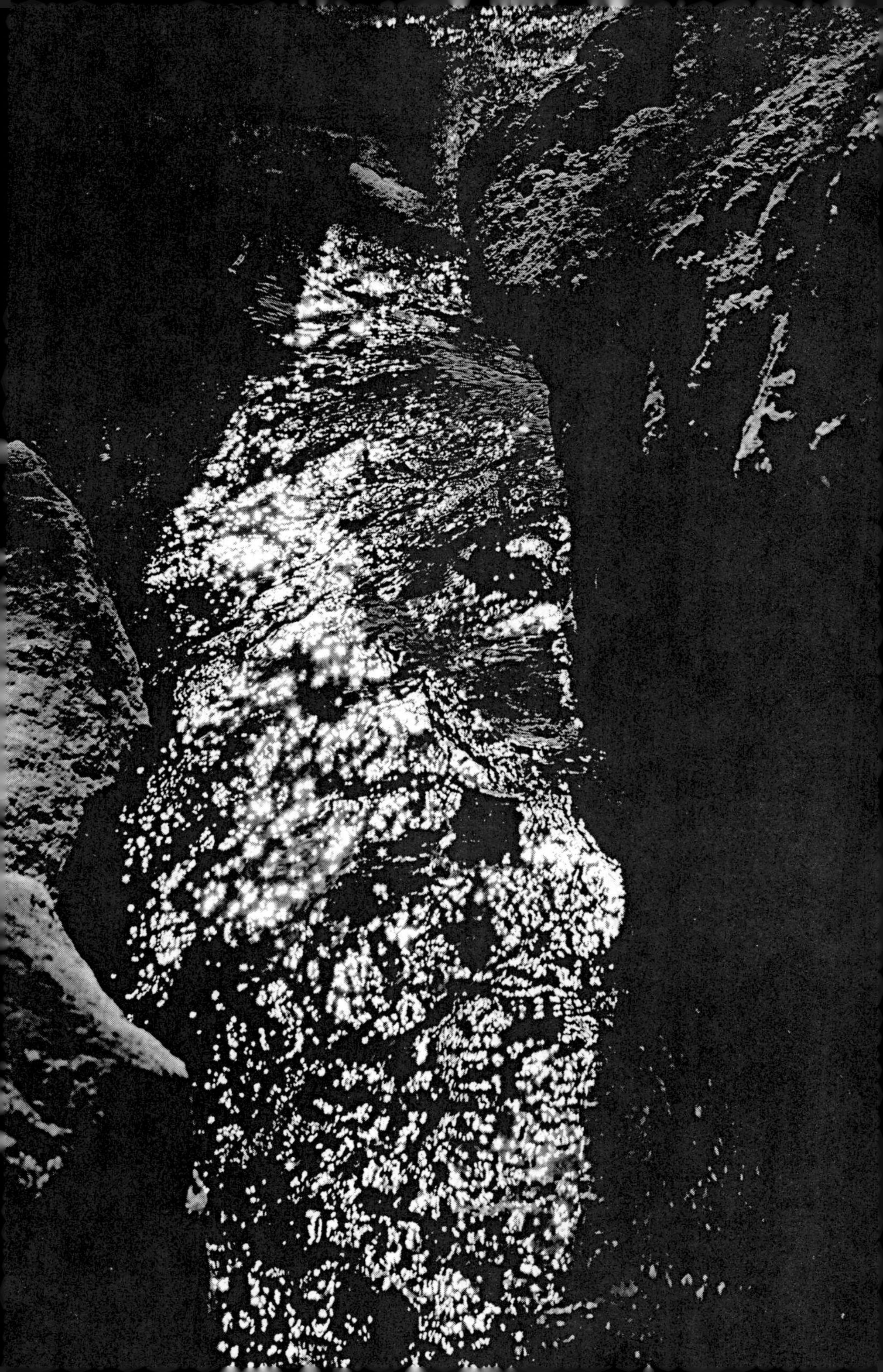

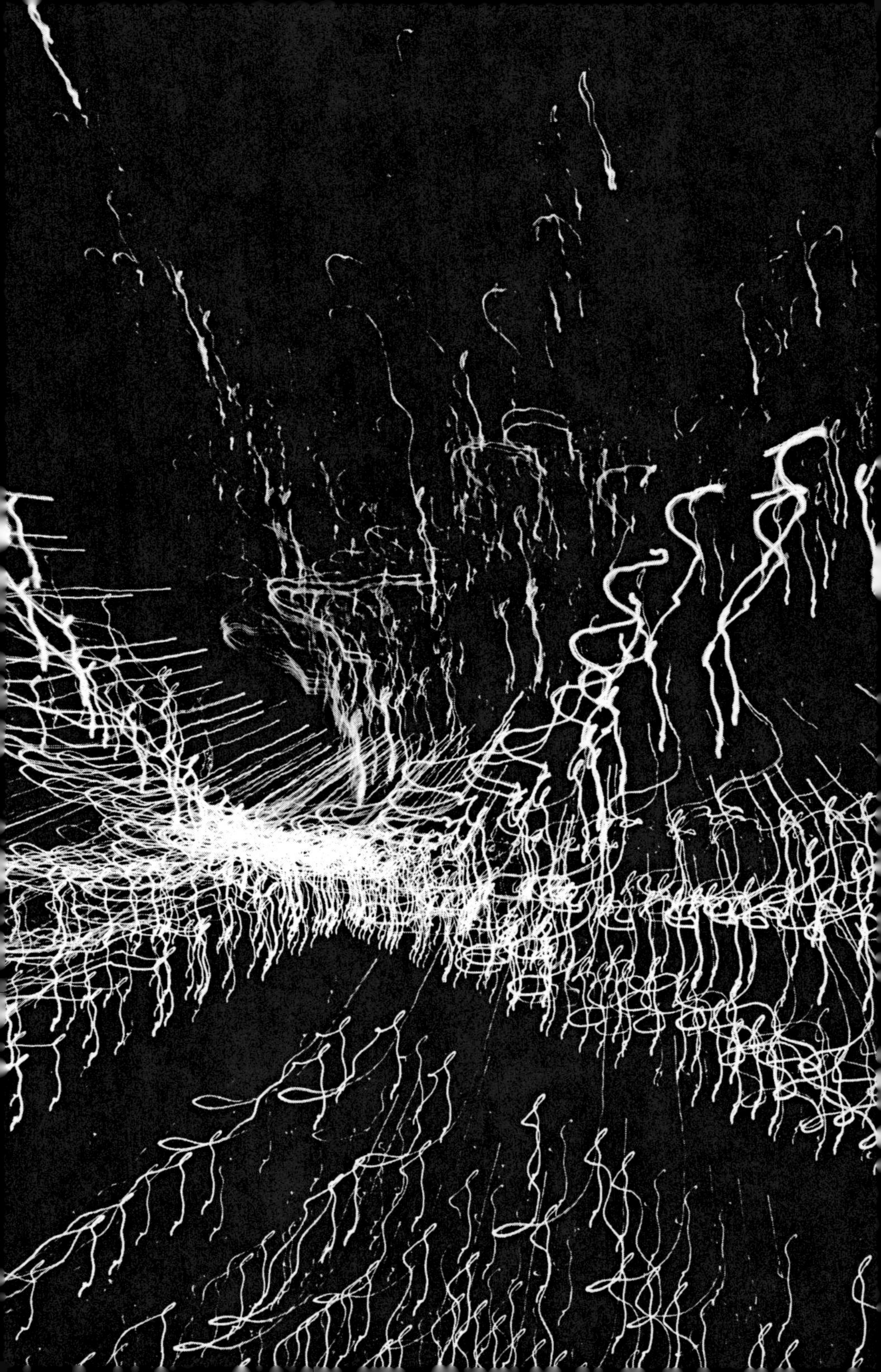

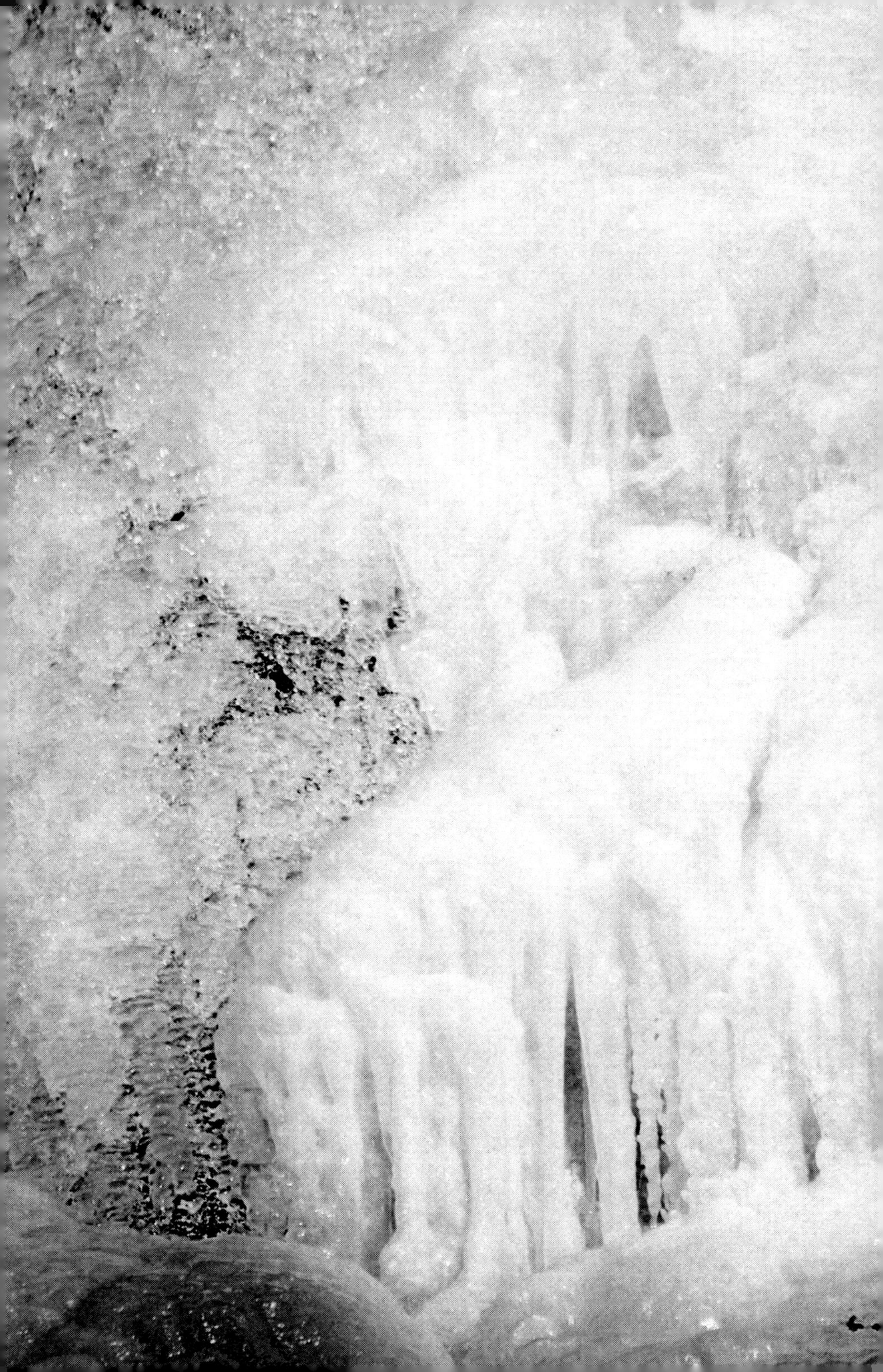

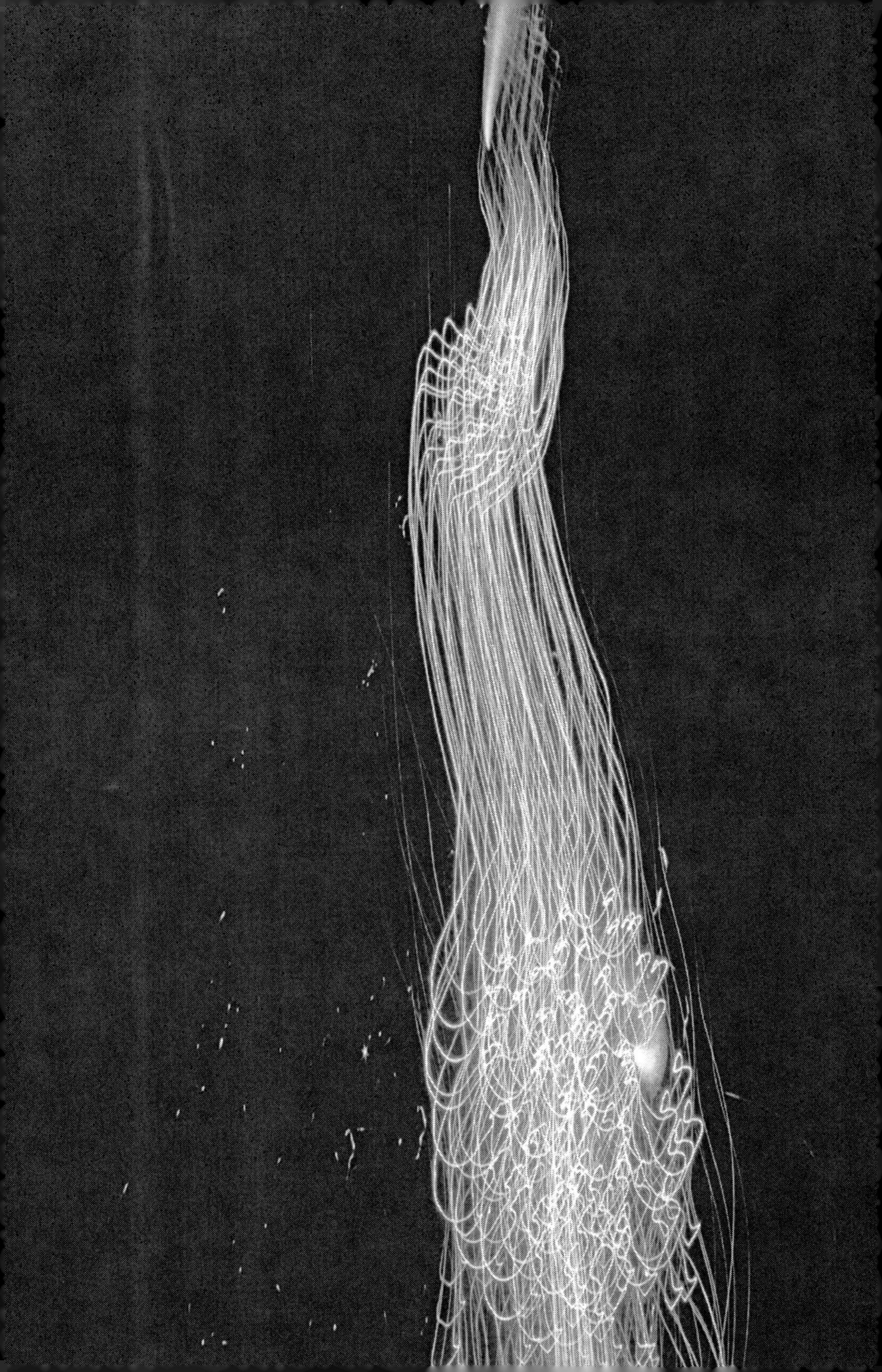

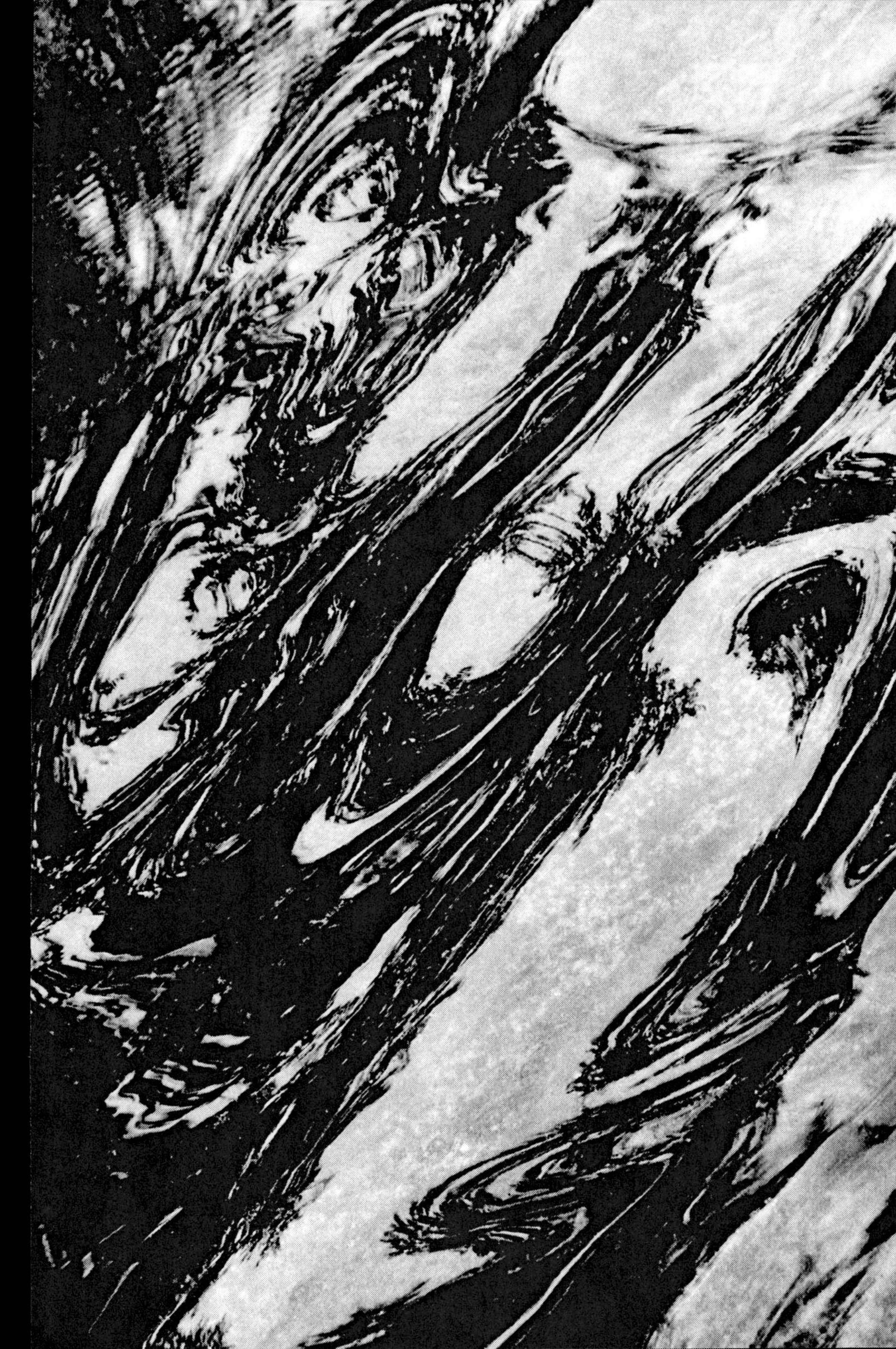

this   moment
          and
all
          the ones
to come
          but oh!
                    how very
unique
          each
one can be
          some are dancing
others are mourning
          this one so sweet
that one bitter
          some brilliant blood red
some dull cold metal
          but this one
                    Ahhhhhhhh!
                              black sable silence

-

now
I am
on my deathbed
it could happen
just like that
          l o n g

and
a g o n I z I n g l y
            s l o w
or
        dot dot dot
        just like that!
here   one moment
gone   the next
but   gone where
exactly
            no
one   really knows
but   perhaps
                that's not
        the question
to be answered
. . . the mystery is
                how   do   I
live love
        now
-

now
        rocking
and
                            gliding
back

and forth
side to side
watching the scent
	of the incense rise
silver blue streamers
	curl and unfurl
as the candle wax melts
in
	the light of the flame
silence	resounds
and
	still
thoughts remain
	Peace	Peace	Peace
This IS the now of rest
-
this is the now
	that sighs
and still wonders
	how and why
this is the now
	that is broken
this one made whole
	this is the now
I confess
	yes
I made many mistakes

NOW

　　　but I did my best
this is the now
　　　I keep learning as I go
what it means to be me
　　　how to hear
how to see
　　　what to do
what to say
　　　how to make my way
with each moment
　　　of every night
and all
　　　the days
-
this is the now
when I have
nothing
to say
"nothing."
-
now is not
the time to ask
what it means
how or why
now is　　　not　　the time
to make money phone calls
text

not the time
to strategize and plan
now is the time to close my eyes
place my hand on my heart
take a breath
and let it go
with a smile and a sigh
while   time   glides
into
the   community of   the   past
-
is each now
up
to you
will it work out
just as you wanted
just as you planned
or
a tragic disaster land
(let's hope not)
it might be a surprise
even better than
you imagined
or   could have hoped for
this one   a dream come true
that one   a drop dead knock out
and many more to blow your mind ones to

NOW

come
so follow your heart
    whichever way it plays out
        learn to trust that
-
now
 I wonder
now I worry
now
I   rest
now   I turn my gaze
inside
as breath rises
and subsides
now
church bells chime
I open my eyes
see a guy biking by
the new mint leaves
reaching for the sky
as they make love with the breeze
what will arise
now
church bells
continue to chime
I turn to my heart
hum an ancient melody

stop wondering
how or why
where it is all going
what to do next
for now is
the time
to   simply   abide
-
now
this   this
        Holy Longing
                to be One with the Tide*
            and
    this   holding
back
        holding   tight
        but
there is
                (I reluctantly realize)
nothing
to hold on to
                not even
a railing
                suspended in a void
as I dreamed
years ago
when I saw

the Golden Temple
        in the vast pristine blue sky
oh
    what am I going on about?
holding on to thoughts
      following them
here and there
when I'm supposed to be following my
breath
    and letting them go
where do they lead
    where is there to go?
only a way from here
      a way from now
yet they ramble on
some times a wild goose chase
some times they lead me home
    they make me laugh
and lead to tears
      play hide and seek
until silence returns
now   NOW   now
-

now
taking a twilight stroll
with my thoughts
they always seem to find their way

to tag along
but ironically
it always seems
I wind up
following them
off we go
to unknown lands
some times I need
a traffic cop
in a top hat
it's one round about
after another
but after all
I always wind up
here
now
-
now
basking in the bath
with Yo Yo Ma's Bach cello suites
meandering their way
note by note
the medley fades
now barely audible
as my mind
takes a detour
through a construction zone

and branches out
in a vast valley
possibilities
endless
but now
I return to the Sound pulsing
in my body
as the tide rolls in
slides out
through and around
this heart and soul
while the bow
vibrates my strings
just for now
-
now
      I'm thinking about this
now
      how about that?
the ever continual conversations
        gossip
     "what he said"
     "what she did"
and then
      the conversation
      between my breath
        and my body

NOW

NOWNOWNOWNOWNOWNOWNOWNOWNOW NOWNOWNOWNOWNOWNOWNOWNOWNOW

neurons firing
hormones brewing
blood flowing
alveoli alchemy
seeing and hearing
my restless mind
                why
do you keep wandering off
      when deep down
          you know
how you love
        to rest
in the arms
     on the breast
of still nest
-

now
some precious moments
with a very dear old soul friend
our joy
hearing each other's voice
laughter bubbles over
deep listening
a treasure always
-

now
I am remembering

when we first met
your palm on my shoulder
the way my head turned
in slow motion
my chin leading the way
my eyes following close behind
to gaze into the face of an angel
your long strawberry blonde hair
curtaining your emerald green eyes
the gentle curve
of your forehead
the sweep of your nose
especially the gift of your smile
truly love at first sight
and despite our human foibles
always love
I feel you with me now
24 years after you really sprouted wings
and flew on
but
oh the longing for your laughter
longing for our tears
sharing our hopes and fears
I still see your face
and the look in your eyes
silk screened on my heart
oh glorious

epiphany of light that you are
Tajalli*

-

now
5 a.m.
why am I awake?
was it the chocolate
is it you Beloved
who whispers in my inner ear
"open your eyes
see the dawn's silver blue hue
that's Me!
you know"
now is the time
to meet and greet
our new day
no need to tremble
no need to shake and shiver
simply lie back
float on the gentle tide
rest your gaze on the waxing pastel blue sky
the horizon beyond
where sea and sky embrace
a thin silver sliver
that goes forever
One Breath

NOW

-

now
as I try to relax
soothe my troubled mind
always needing to remind me
        this world is a dangerous place
some say it is all Maya*
        illusion
do not be fooled
    like the quail mistaking a reflection
                            for reality
a trick of light
        on a rain soaked sun
                streaming morning
it thought it saw a tree and winged its way
        but alas it was only glass
how was she to know
                and in a flash it lay lifeless
on the ground
        If it only could see it was only
                a reflection
                not reality

-

now and then
        now slides into then
and   then   becomes   when
                and

then   there's   here
          that somehow
                    turns into there
time and sapce
                              God Herself
the water we swim in
could it be
                    this world
                              a womb
dying a birth canal
-
now
I don't know about you
so I am feeling a little shy
to admit
sometimes
my life, all life
truly seems quite surreal
I mean
picture this
here I am on a Sunday morning
doing my laundry
on a planet
the size of an atom
in a galaxy among 100 million galaxies
orbiting around the sun
with so many other planets

while we are orbited by the moon
that guides the tides
and waxes and wanes
and all of that
breath flows in and out
heart beats
blood flows
and on and on it goes
as I turn the dials
Pour the laundry detergent in
and turn the water on
close the lid
and go on with my day
now

-

now
a prayer
a prayer of peace
a prayer o glorification and thanks giving
a prayer of loons at sunset in the backwoods
of Algonquin
a prayer of humility
humbled by earthquakes
volcanos and tornados
a prayer of sanctification
a prayer for redemption
Holy Holy Holy

NOW NOWNOWNOWNOWNOWNOWNOWNOWNOWNOW

NOWNOWNOWNOWNOWNOWNOWNOWNOWNOW

-

now
on this new mint green dandelion yellow
powder blue sky spring dawn
I wave in the breeze
amid the tall grass and aspen trees
in the middle of the meadow in the shelter
of blossoming snow white dogwoods and
lavender lilac trees
my pollen flying
hither and yon
with hummingbirds and bees
all through summer's shine
what will this autumn's harvest bring forth
to celebrate
                    I know!
whatever seeds I sow
and tend will grow
come thanksgiving
may all be nutritious and delicious
-

now
infinite possibilities
lie in wait
turn this way
follow that one
this one thought

that one idea
where might it lead
will it turn the
corner
into another dimension
to startle you
or will it vanish
slide by
sink into the dark recesses of your mind
or will you plant it
a seed
in a secret garden
in your heart
to gestate stir grow restless
throb root sprout
grow green and wild
-
now what possibility
will arise
to sprout wings and fly
no rush no push
some thing is bound to happen
words will appear
and go skipping across the page
perhaps to land in your heart
a name
a memory

a desire
that has been only a spark
now fanned by this breath
to burst into flame
bring a smile to your face
-

now
      I see you
now I don't
      a game of
            hide and seek
is that you Beloved
      I hear you speak sweet words of love
your song rings so true
      a lullaby to heal my heart and sooth
my soul
is that your caress
      in the steaming hot shower
            a cascade
      baptizing my breasts
is that you Beloved
      guiding my hand
            Yes
I know that scent
      that perfume
      unlike no other

-

Beloved
now
I come to be with you
and you   Alone
in silence and solitude
for it is with you
that my heart is healed
my soul soothed
yet I cannot see your face
I do not even know your name
you are all things everywhere
it is not in doing my taxes
or surfing the net
that I feel close to you
I see you in butterflies
feel you in the warm summer breeze
when I close my eyes
turn my gaze inside
where You Alone
abide

-

now
the cusp of possibility again
letting my self slide into reverie
no need to be on guard
or sound and alarm

savor this silience
but to be perfectly honest
it would be so much easier
if you were here
lying next to me
I would curl my cat body into your arms
rest my head on your hear
as you plant a kiss seed
on my temple
so tender
a little prayer
a beautiful blessing
a treasure
to cherish
-
take a moment
now
invoke
reach down to molten ground
call forth
the Hidden One
She has secrets to sound
stories to share
I never know with Her
what will She think of next
She's full of surprises
She has innumerable disguises

but if you close your eyes
lie very still
you will see
Her true countenance
always shines through
Her Mona Lisa smile
to dazzle and beguile
-
now
dusk deepens
cumulus clouds
so light white fluffy
now
steel grey
heavy and ominous
chill winds
brush leaves
branches bow and bend
knocking on my cottage wall
thunder a distant hum
rolling over the Great Divide
announcing its arrival
with lightening and rain
to wash away all pain
until night turns to day
and the sun reign on high

-

now
a prayer for Maggie
beloved Maggie
how i long to hold you
close
to my bare breast
stroke your belly
run my fingers through your thick pitch
black coat
feel you stretch and curl
while i scratch behind your ear
feel you purr with pure pleasure
but alas
i fear it is not meant to be
I so wish i knew why
it seems you hold so much inside
for at any moment
you might bear your claws
eyes bulging
eye teeth showing
screeching like an owl
if only I could soothe your soul
suck out the venum that poisons your heart
pollutes your mind
and then bathe you with love

-

now
I awake and
reach for you
but you are not here
I slip back into sleep
awake again
longing to feel you
snuggle and spoon me
stroke my hair
feel your lips
graze my back
as I turn and
rest my head on your shoulder
your arms wrapped all
around me
belly to belly
heart with heart
I tilt my head
my eyes reach out of sleep
smile softly
to see your new moon
eyes
slivers
in the sky of your radiant face
our lips
magnets

drawn toward each other
meet
ignite the day
and propel us
on our own special way
-
is this the One?
The One
Moment
or is it
....
this One
each to its own
now
-
it's all so very
fragile
right now
fragile and immense
miniscule and
inconceivable
unknowably vast
I close my eyes
take a breath
stand firmly
arms outstretched
come on Life

what's it going to be
this now
-
it is
dusk now
as I walk around
my old cottage
drawing the blinds
turning on the lamps
like the gentle closing of a book
just finished
there is
a special quality
in the luminous silver silence
of dusk
no matter how
the day
and sunset have gone
I gaze out the window
one last time
at this day passing by
a steel blue grey
metallic cast
on the snow
and the chill of the still
air
carries me into   night

–

now
lying under the old apple tree
a tableau of such a brilliant
blue diamond sky above
gentle breeze caressing my face
pink blossoms
a celebration
resurrection
redemption
at the gate of the Promise land
sweet aromas
to heal my shatterered and battered nerves
and heart
the divine plan
and I the star of Her play
if ony I had the script
it seems to be all improvisation
but I open to guidance
I feel you take my hand
together *we* step across the threshold
taste the milk and honey
float in serene pools of healing waters
truly the goddess' garden of pure de-light
Liberte
all praise and gratitude

-

now
instead of
weeping and worrying
instead of
catastrocphzing
instead of
pushing and shoving my way
through the day
instead of this
instead of that
I sit back
and bask in the bizarreness of it all
shake my head in wonder and awe
I think of my grandson's giggles
my grand daughter's sweet baby scent
her chubby arms and little feet
my lover's embrace
I arise with a song
in my heart
Kali Durga Shakti-ma*
I dance spin around and around
until I stop
and the world spins on
-

now
a full moon

early spring night
in my garden
of pure delight
fireflies flicker
stars twinkle
silence echoes
with all Her might
while earth worms dig
beneath the comforter of holy ground
seeds sprout
roots stretch
the sun glows brighter
day by day kale grows green
lilacs and irises bloom
I sing in my hammock
chocolate melts in my mouth
a prayer in my heart
a song on my lips
"Holy Holy Holy!"
-
now
I see
I walk around the gallery
my boots clicking along the floor
my eyes graze the wall
I see
a grove of aspen trees

their mint green silver dollar leaves
shimmering in the sunlight
I place myself
in the painting
now a young girl
with long curly auburn hair
escaping from a robin's egg blue bonnet
tied with a ruby satin ribbon
lounging on a grassy mound
seranaded by swallow's song
a sound so sweet
I can taste it
laughter and love
hand in hand
meander their way
a bubbling brook
splatters and splashes
such a splendid day!
-
now
I see you
all blue
your black eyes
looking back at me
your chin
resting on your fist
what is it?

is there something you wish to say
you don't look that happy
a touch sad
 a bit of an edge
in the crease of your brow
a question
a secret
in your eyes
what could it be?
"why oh why?"
"what to do now?"
a desperate plea
"please help me!"
what it is
I say back to you
"come rest your head
settle in my embrace
let me turn blue to red
soothe your troubled mind
unfurl your fist
and plant a kiss
-

now
a Voice is calling
in me
to me
deep inside a well

    the call
silently resounding
still
I can barely hear it
I can only imagine
who
   it is
   telling me important secrets
yet the chatter
     the clatter
of the ticking
   of the clock
the screams of bombs and sirens
       wails of hungry babies
     sighs of lonely people
    moaning and groaning
shaking and quaking of Mother Earth
    and the grapplng
     and the sorting in my mind
is so compelling
   claws grasping
pleading
   "don't turn away!"
and You, Beloved!
    beckoning open arms
warm heart   om
     Home!

-

now is time for Praise
to the one who inspires me
the one who keeps me safe
the one who holds me back
the one who breaks free
the courage to be
the voices that praise
the whispers that betray
the love that saves
the ties that bind
the heart that breaks
the soul that knows
the mind that thinks
eyes that see
ears that hear
lips that kiss
dancing feet
sun shine
moon light
rainbows

-

now

we women are calling
SHOUTING OUT
to our sisters and brothers
to all others'

hearts hands and minds
     to set all our judgments and criticisms
aside
     to take a stand
       to join hands
and sing and dance
     to give Mother Earth and all
          Her creatures
our children a chance
     to turn curses into blessings
to plant our soul seeds
     in our Garden of Earth
we women cry and wail
     in pain, in rapture
our waters break
     with faith courage perseverance
         we give birth
we will not let life falter and fail
we – women
     celebrate our Sovereignty
–

now
we stand
waves of women
side by side
shoulder to shoulder
hand in hand

NOW NOWNOWNOWNOWNOWNOWNOWNOWNOWNOW

NOWNOWNOWNOWNOWNOWNOWNOWNOW

heart to heart
                    NOW AND ALL WAYS
        stepping through time
each a wave
                    cresting
rising
                            flowing
        falling
over the shore of
oppression and lies
doubt and fear
        the tide comes in
the tide goes out
        spashing away the grains of sand
that seem to stand in our way
while the undertoe
                sucks them back to sea
to be taken into a shell
                    one by one
until   a pearl   is   born
        wave   upon   wave
grain upon grain
        shell after shell
pearls together
        alone in our shells
mother   daughter   mother   daughter
        from ancient priestess

 to corporate lawyer
amazon queen to single mother
                              witch to bag lady
Sappho to Maya Angelou
who ever questions that the ocean lives
              forever?
-

now
spraying and splashing
your love crashes over me
the surf
at evening tide
rushing in
from some great deep vastness
spraying and splashing
sometimes the swell froths,
swallows a boulder
for a moment
or two
it gleams
more brightly
-

now I understand
the crone sacrifices outer beauty
for inner radiant truth and wisdom
Grandmother Wisdom
Sophia Wisdom

the butterfly metamorphozied
into a Great Horned Owl
who sees 180 degrees around
through the black veil of night
may it be so!
-

noq
the sun watches
as it makes its way
to celebrate the meeting of
air and water
on the long thin line called horizon
do rock outcroppings tremble within
as i do?
when waves bear down upon them
do they beg for entry, dissolving
while holding on to the way they seem al-
ways to have been?
i want to soak you up
as sand soaks you up
-

will it take an earthquake
to shatter memory
or
          simply time
how many days months years
                    year after year

-

now the sound of your voice
lingers in my heart
like melted dark chocolate
the brush of your lips
languishes on my breast
your sweet scent wafts with each breath
I cloak my eyes
feel your gaze on my face
as I curl
snug in your warm embrace
until sleep carries me
through the cold dark winter night
-

now I'm thinking about respect
even a little consideration
to begin with
simple decency
just sayin'
and then there's preciousness
handle with care
fragile
delicate
and moving on to sacredness
reverence
awe and the ultimate
Holy Now

–

finally now
the scent of Russian olive trees
surprises and delights me
as it does every June
here in my Rocky mountain home town
the grey green leaves
adorned with blossoms
if you've never had the pleasure
close your eyes
and think Jasmine
take a slow full breath
and imagine!
–

now I see Her
almost all light
ephemeral
halo aglow
shimmering across the threshold
of time and space
I'm right behind
about to glide over
a new world
a new life
gazing in awe
leaning toward
I know She knows

I'm there
yet she does not look back
She says not a word
nor utters any sound
"follow my lead"
like a magnet
i am carried forward
"follow   my lead"
my heart beats
FOLLOW   my lead
FOLLOW   my lead
where else
would i want to be
no reason to resist
She would not lead me astray
surely She will guide me
Home
to the Promise Land
now
-
now
I wonder
if there's anything
I can do or say
to ease your pain
and help you on your way
how about…

I know what it is
to hurt
to be angry sad and alone
to ache over a mistake
confused about it all
to shiver and quake for
a warm hand to hold
a loving face to behold
for a special someone
to look you in the eye
and say:
"I'm here through it all!"
-

now
I am
now
I am
not
-

now
I enfold myself
in angel wings
nestle into Her breast
give thanks
to the one
the only
great Now

NOW

-

Postscript

now
aLL
we are left with
is the question
how will we live this now
the only now we have
each now
a foundation for the next
-
now
all I have left
to say
is
I invite you
to write
your now

Give it a try. Keep a little notebook or your
phone or tablet with you and take a minute or
two a few times a day to write "Now.... ' And see
what comes. See how it feels, how does doing it
impact you?
open to surprises. If nothing is coming, write
"now nothing is coming" or "I don't Know what
to say" or start again with the opening phrase.

Below are a few possible starting phrases, al-
though simply starting with the word "Now" is
fine. Also please feel free to add your own to the
list with or without starting with "Now."

Now Prompts:

Prompts are a writing exercise, sometimes considered a warm up. The instructions are to set a timer for 10 minute (you can always restart;) Start writing the phrase: "Now...." And keep writing, no crossing out, no erasing, just keep the pen or keys moving, let what comes come, be

now:

I am	I wish
I Love	Alone
Is	Speak
I want to know	Dance

Write your <u>NOW</u> Here

NOWNOWNOWNOWNOWNOWNOWNOWNOW **NOW** NOWNOWNOWNOWNOWNOWNOWNOWNOW

NOWNOWNOWNOWNOWNOWNOWNOWNOW **NOW** NOWNOWNOWNOWNOWNOWNOWNOWNOW

Refererences

(In alphabetical order)

Aotearoa
 Maori name for New Zealand

Dakini
A Sanscrit word literally meaning "sky goer" or "Sky Dancer."
It is equivalent to Khandro in the Tibetan Buddhist tradi-
tion and has many meanings. Fundamentally Dakinis are
the embodiment of the Divine in Feminine form. There are
peaceful Dakinis and wrathful Dakinis, Women practitioners,
oracles, deities, energies.

Durga
Hindu lore has it that when the Gods were defeated by
the evil ones, they retreated high up in the mountains and
remembered a prophesy that the Goddess Durga will come
to save the world. She comes riding on her tiger, with a
retenue of Dakinis and vanquishes the evil. This myth is ex-
tremely relevant and important in our time. Durga symbol-
izes the wrathful compassion of the feminine that is spiritu-
ally, psychologically and culturally needed to be redeemed
in order for women to stand up to and transform our history
of denigration and abuse and to save our planet from the
patriarchal mindset that is leading us toward devastation.

Fool
The Fool is a figure from the tarot deck.

Gaia
Goddess of Earth

Inanna
Sumarian Queen of the Great Above who journies to the
Underworld to visit her Dark Sister Ereshkigal.

Kali

Kali is another Hindu Goddess. She too represents an aspect of the feminine that has been obliterated from our culture and women's psyches. Kali is the fearful and ferocious form of the mother goddess. She represents the Crone, the Destroyer of all that must die.

Kurukule

Kurukule is a red semi-wrathful Dakini. Goddess of Power. Powerful, red in color with one face, hair flowing upward, three eyes and four hands, slightly fierce in expression, she holds a bow and arrow in the first pair of hands and a hook and lasso in the lower pair. All the hand objects are constructed of red utpala flowers and are used as implements for the subjugation and accomplishment of all goals.

Neytiri

In the film, Avatar, Neytiri is a Navi Princess Neytiri, a revered young powerful sacred woman.
http://james-camerons-avatar.wikia.com/wiki/Neytiri

Sangre de Christos pass

Spanish for blood of Christ – a beautiful mountain range in New Mexico and Colorado.

Shakti

Shakti is a mysterious physical psychospiritual force in some ways related to Kundalini. The female principle of divine energy, especially when personified as the supreme deity. It is the concept, or personification, of divine feminine creative power, sometimes referred to as 'The Great Divine Mother' in Hinduism. Not only is Shakti responsible for creation, it is also the agent of all change. Shakti is cosmic existence as well as liberation.

Shiva
In Hinduism, Shiva is partner to Shakti, the male principle
and the one part of the trinity, the Destroyer along with
Vishnu, the Preserver, and Brahma, the Creator.
Lord of the dance and Lord of death.

Sophia
Means "wisdom" in Greek. Intuitive Embodied feminine
wisdom. She is often portrayed with an owl on her shoulder.
It is from this name that we have the word philosophy.

Tajalli, Crowning glory of light, epiphany of light

About the Author

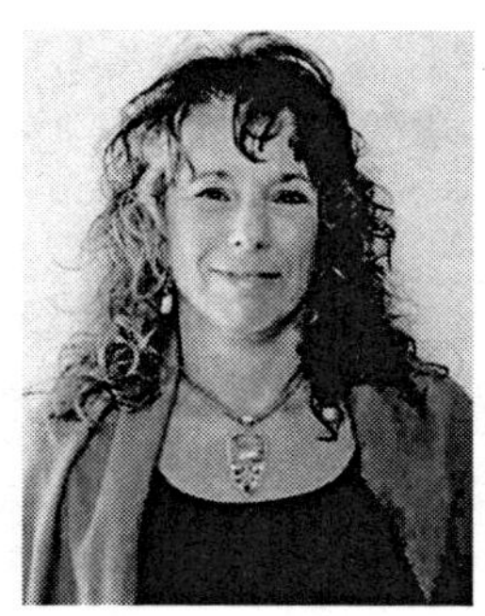

Dakini Lynn Marlow has been on a healing journey her entire adult life. After many "nows" growing up in the heart of New York City, she ventured out in the world, living in Taiwan, Canada, and a spiritual community, as well as traveling to many other countries. Her inner journey is both vast and deep as well. She has immersed herself in Sufism, Buddhism, Jungian work, Diamond Heart work, and the Sacred Feminine to name a few of her explorations. She has been ordained as an interfaith minister, guide, and retreat guide in the Sufi Order International. She is a massage therapist, working in a variety of modalities, e.g. Biodynamic cranial sacral work, Reiki, breathwork, and integrative work. As a psychotherapist, she has been able to draw from and integrate the wisdom and healing she has gleaned from all her life experience, study and training to help many, especially women, on their healing journey. Dakini has taught internationally and welcomes invitations to travel and teach. She is a lover of life, all forms of creativity and she especially loves to dance!

Dakini lives in Boulder, Colorado where she spends her time writing, making art, out in nature with her camera, teaching, doing healing work, and dancing!

Email her to find out about her and her work.
lynnmarlow@comcast.net

CPSIA information can be obtained
at www.ICGtesting.com
Printed in the USA
FSOW02n2057250417
33565FS